# Rocks Rock

*Rough and Tumbled, Colorful and Cool
Rocks and Minerals*

## Brenda DeHaan

~ 1 ~

DeHaan, Brenda

Rocks Rock: Rough and Tumbled, Colorful and Cool Rocks and Minerals

1. Rocks and minerals 2. Geology 3. Mineralogy 4. Science 5. Nature
552

# Introduction

Rocks rock! Learning about them is cool! This book includes

- Interesting crystals
- Why rocks are different colors
- Natural and carved shapes and designs
- How rocks help people's lives
- Fun facts and photos

Rocks, stones, minerals, and crystals are so intertwined that these words will be used in a more general sense.

In short, a **crystal** is a solid structure where atoms form in a certain geometric pattern like a repeating lattice. A **mineral** has natural chemicals that form in nature. Minerals can change the colors of crystals. A **rock** or **stone** can have a variety of minerals in it. Most rocks are millions or even billions of years old.

# Let's Get Rockin'!

One of the most common rocks starts with the letter *q*. No matter where you live, your neighborhood surely has some. Do you know what it is?

The answer is quartz. Did you get it right?

You probably aren't going to find a cool-looking quartz cluster like in the picture above, but quartz is all over the place in various shapes and shades.

Some clear quartz are as transparent (clear) as glass. Some are translucent where you can see light through them, but not details. Others are opaque where you cannot see through them at all. Some are small while others are huge.

What is this man doing to the rock? He has
a hammer and a chisel to break open the geode
to see what might be inside.

Here are the interiors of geodes. It takes thousands of years for crystals to form inside certain rocks that have pockets of air and water or other fluids inside.

Some geodes have different colors inside because they were exposed to different minerals while they formed.

The outside of a geode looks nothing like its interior. Geodes with purple crystals inside are usually amethyst. Geodes with yellow inside may be citrine. Until you break open a geode, you won't know what you may find. It's a surprise! It might be an agate or an agate with quartz.

# Rough and Tumbled

If you buy a rock that is smooth and glossy, it probably had been tumbled. If you find a rock near a lake or river that is smooth, that was a natural process from rolling in water or through erosion. These types of rocks can slowly get smaller and smaller and might even end up as sand.

Rock tumblers mimic this rolling action. An electric barrel filled with grit (like sand), water, and rough rocks rotates for weeks. Eventually, the rough textures becomes smooth.

Some people prefer rough stones while others like tumbled rocks better.

The sodalite on the left is rough; the one of the right is a tumbled stone.

The geodes are natural, the smooth stones were tumbled, and the more textured stones are rough. The shades of purple vary because of their varying mineral contents.

# Colorful and Cool

Minerals affect rocks' colors. Iron can cause red, orange, or purple hues. Magnesium can cause black shades. Nickel, chromium, and copper add green colors. Blue might also be from copper. Many factors can affect each rock's color, but mineral content is a big reason.

Jasper can be red, yellow, green, and a mixture of other colors.

Some turquoise looks green while other specimens appear blue. Different locations have different minerals in the area which affect the hues. Can you tell which stones had been tumbled and which had not?

Quartz can be clear, purple (amethyst), yellow (citrine), pink (rose quartz), orange (carnelian), green (aventurine), or shades of gray (smokey quartz). It's like they're cousins on the Silicon Dioxide family tree. Minerals change the colors, but everyone in the quartz family has silicon dioxide.

Not every stone is quartz on the tree in the picture. See if you can figure out which ones are. (Look for clear quartz, citrine, and aventurine.)

Calcite is a softer stone that comes in many colors. It feels almost waxy. Some of it is translucent, but other calcites are opaque. The largest piece on the right side is called rainbow calcite because it has numerous layers of color.

From the variety of crystals below, which color is your favorite?

Not only are crystals cool to look at, they feel naturally cool (unless the sun is warming them).

# Natural and Carved Designs

Shapes like hearts, animals, and stars are popular. Sometimes you may find a rock that looks like a heart, but most of the time they are carved.

This crazy lace agate heart is naturally shaped and has interesting patterns.

The larger amethyst heart has a natural heart shape while the 3 smaller geodes were cut into hearts.

Some stones are soft while others are harder. They are rated on Mohs Hardness Scale which helps in knowing what something may be used for. Talc is very soft and is rated a 1. Quartz is a 7 while diamond has the hardest rating of 10. The lower the number, the more easily the rock can chip or break. If carving a stone, it has to be hard enough to not crumble and fall to pieces but soft enough to be able to carve

It may look like one of the aquamarines was carved, but it is its natural shape.

All these hearts were carved. The top one is red jasper, the grayish one is smokey quartz, and the multi-colored one is polychrome jasper. Blue calcite is in the middle with pyrite next to it and rose quartz below it.

The horse and bunny were carved from tiger's eye, a stone that has a natural reflective shine called *chatoyancy*.

Some rocks are older than dinosaurs.

Soapstone and Mexican onyx are soft enough for carving and make interesting animals. The tumbled pink stones are rose quartz. The green are amazonite and aventurine. The blue are lapis lazuli above the dinosaur's tail and labradorite on the right side.

You are wise enough to know which chrysocolla stone was carved and which ones were not.

The top star is moss agate, then blue goldstone, red jasper, snowflake obsidian and sodalite. (Goldstone is manmade with copper. It may be gold, blue, or green.) Below are two pieces of moss agate, one carved and one tumbled.

The blue angel is carved from angelite. The other stones are tumbled angelite.

If you like the color soft blue, this might be the stone for you.

These flower designs are all natural. The reddish barite rose cluster is fragile because it has a lot of sand in it. The geode has a very unique filling that looks like flower petals. The amethyst rose also resembles a flower and is not your typical amethyst.

Wavellite has radiating clusters that resemble green flowers. This rock contains aluminum. It is a soft, more fragile crystal, only 3.5-4 on the Mohs Hardness scale. Many people have never seen or heard of wavellite.

The delicate fern designs are not painted or carved. The dendrites result from cracks that get filled with iron or manganese oxide.

Rose quartz usually does not have dendrites. This one was found in the Black Hills of South Dakota. The rock below is a dendritic agate.

The flower petal design on the sand dollar is still visible after turning into a fossil.

Petrified wood is also known as fossilized wood. It is easy to recognize when it still looks like wood but is as hard as a rock—because it is a rock!

# Ways We Use Rocks

Rocks have made life easier for as long as people have been alive.

Long ago Native Americans made arrowheads for hunting and for weapons. Not all arrowheads are old; people still flint nap stones today as a hobby.

Nowadays, some people use diamond drill bits with industrial quality diamonds, not the gem quality stones.

Rubies and diamonds may be used in laser lights. Again, these are not the gem quality stones. Rocks have different grading scales which helps determine their best uses.

Quartz vibrates at a steady rate of 32,768 times per second. When you see *quartz* on a watch or a clock, it is because quartz was used in creating the timepiece. This watch has tiger's eye on its band and quartz inside to keep time.

Quartz is also used in computers, radios, microphones, ultrasound machines, and other electronic equipment.

Rocks are used in making roads and sidewalks. These large quartzite stones stop cars from accidentally driving into the river. Smaller quartzite and quartz may be used for paths or driveways.

Landscape blocks look good in yards, and cats may enjoy them also. Many are concrete made from small rocks bound together.

An even bigger project than landscaping is building a building with stones.

When we salt our food, we are eating crystals. Halite is usually just called *salt*. Pink Himalayan salt has become more common in eating and as decorative salt lamps.

Jewelry is another common use of crystals. Look around and see how many people are wearing gemstone jewelry. Some pieces are wire-wrapped where the wire goes outside of the stone. Gemstone beads have holes made before you purchased them.

There's just something special about rocks. Whether you find rocks where you live or buy them in stores or online, each one is different. Each one is unique.

Whether you use rocks for a certain purpose or just like them because they feel cool and comforting in your hand, each rock you own has meaning.

Rocks allow you to experience nature in a different way. Rocks can make you smile. Rocks rock!

# About the Author

Brenda DeHaan is a K-12 librarian who loves rocks and reading. She hopes that you do also. This amethyst geode cathedral is the largest rock in her collection.

## Children's Picture Books by Brenda DeHaan

*ABC Amazing Book of Crystals*

*Crystals for Kids: Learn the Names of 17 Rocks and Minerals*

*The Flower Fairies Meet the Talking Rainbow Rocks*

*Beach Surprise: Unicorns, Mermaids, Flower Fairies, and Rainbow Rocks Meet at the Beach*

*Hooray for a Fun Day!*

*Rocks with Socks and Fox*

*Rocks and Rhyme 2 in 1 Fun*

*Adventures with Apollo: The Cat Who Rules Rooftops*

*Abenteuer mit Apollo*

*Cat Naps, Dog Naps: Who Naps More?*

*From Apple to Zombie Drawing Challenge: Illustrate Your Own Halloween Book*

*From Angel to Zzzz's Drawing Challenge*

## For Tweens and Teens

*Shine Life a Crystal: 12 Quick Tips to Rock Life*

*Life Advice for Teens from an Ageless Grandma: Tips and Encouragement Just for You*